Single Black Female Addicted to College

50 things I learned in college, while maintaining my happiness & discovering my purpose.

By

Vett Vandiver

Acknowledgements

"For with **God**, nothing is impossible."

Thank you Daddy & Mama for loving me, encouraging me, and supporting me – *regardless*. Love you forever.

Kors, Fraanje, Kyra, Kim, Jerrin, aunts & uncles, cousins, Nick, Brandon, Shayla, Jade, Hannah, Sharena, Shelby, Chris, Alex, Tyler, Eran, Kate, Kia, Erika, Alison, Ellie, Ericka, Jasmine, Bethany, Jonathan, Friendship Baptist Church, Ebenezer Baptist Church, Ms. Milsted, Mr. Veal, GT WBB, Georgia Tech community, Peachtree Ridge High School, B.B. Harris Elementary and Atlanta – thank you, **I love you**.

To the **readers** – I hope you learn something new and that this book prepares for you for some of the **greatest** years of your life.

Education is so very important. We should **never** stop learning.

2

3

 Introduction

Succeeding in life is all about **risks**.

This book is partially my collegiate biography – a look into the past few years of my life that I've spent in college (at Georgia Tech). And, it is also partially a guide to navigating college life as a minority student at a predominately white school and/or a student studying something different than the majority of the school.

I've read and heard about plenty of sugar coated advice books; tips on going to college for the first time…you know, written for "everybody." Yeah, those **never** really helped me. I figured out how to map out my classes and make my schedule the way I wanted, but it took me such a long time to figure out how to become a respected student leader on campus, not just a "black leader."

Although this is my story of being a black student at Georgia Tech, a school where black students are around 6% of the student population, I believe that any person – minority **or** majority – can and **will** relate to my words. Here are **50** pieces of advice from me to you. I've learned that if you want to write something universal, you must write it specifically about **yourself**.

4

Table of Contents

Set goals.

The worst thing you could do is go to college "just to be going," and without any real dreams, hopes, or goals that you plan to accomplish during your time at school. You don't need a perfect list or even a list at all, but have a solid idea of why you want to further your education. For me, I wanted to grow as a person and increase my knowledge by meeting new people from new places. I had dreams of attending a challenging school and excelling at that school.

I planned to join organizations that I was involved in during high school and join organizations that I never thought I'd be involved in. I wanted to be a student leader and achieve academically. I wanted to make an impact at my school and not just be another student walking across the stage at graduation. I wanted to prove wrong my high school teachers who discouraged me. I wanted to make my family proud. I wanted to make myself proud. And I wanted to discover my purpose.

Know why you're attending college.

Registering for classes.

I was involved with Tech's orientation program for two years and
we helped new students register. So… I basically became a registration
expert. My best advice is to plan ahead and have back-up options.
Depending on where you go to school, you may not (probably won't)
get every class that you want every semester. So, plan accordingly, be
flexible and always have other class options for every semester. Most
course options are available on your school's website. I also suggest
getting advice from **older** students about classes, professors, and
course work – but never let this **make or break** your decision.

Me with other Cabinet (orientation) leaders

8

Your first year matters.

In my freshman dorm

What most students say around their third or fourth year of college is, "I wish someone would have told me that freshman year matters." Ok, this is me telling you, **FRESHMAN YEAR MATTERS**.

Sure, you should have fun and enjoy finally getting to college, but please do it responsibly and focus on your academics. My first year in college dropped my GPA pretty low, and raising it over the years has been a challenge. Pay attention when they give advice at your orientation.

Find the balance between socializing, getting involved, schoolwork and everything else. **Balance** and time management are key.

Push yourself.

You'll eventually get accustomed to college life – settle down with a group of friends, find an organization that you fit well with, have a favorite meal at the dining hall. You will become comfortable in your new college environment. But I suggest you push yourself to leave that comfort zone and continue to discover all that your college has to offer.

I can't imagine where I'd be if I had just settled with the people I knew and organizations I was involved in after my second year. Settling can feel good, but can be so dangerous and crippling when you're in an environment with so much potential. Sure, you've already met some cool people, but imagine how many more people are out there waiting to be met. A stranger is just a best friend you've never met.

Pushing yourself also goes for academics and other school-related goals. If you know you'll pass the beginner's Spanish course without any effort, push yourself and sign up for a higher level. Get to know the people in your classes who you normally wouldn't spend time with. I've never challenged myself and regretted it.

10

Stereotypes.

I think that stereotypes will always exists, whether we like them or not. My main issue with stereotypes is when people treat others a certain way based solely on how they look and the generalizations associated with that person's appearance.

As an African American female, I deal with stereotypes (that sometimes lead to discrimination) on a pretty regular basis. At first appearance people may assume I am "ghetto" because I'm black. When I start speaking, people say I talk "white" because I pronounce most of my words correctly. People assume everyone at Georgia Tech is smart. People think I am spoiled because of things that I buy. I've had teachers assume I'm dumb or incapable because of my race. I've had other students assume I have children because I'm a black female. Some stereotypes are good and some are not so fabulous.

My first piece of advice to you: be prepared to be stereotyped in college. When you meet someone new, they will first judge you on your appearance and most likely make generalizations. Second piece: don't do the same.

 Discrimination.

People ask me all the time "what's it like to be black at Tech?" It's interesting. You'll get different answers from different people but I think we all agree that besides the challenges that every student faces, we have an additional set of challenges.

I've heard all types of stories from other black students and black student athletes (at different colleges) – being ignored by their classmates during group assignments, being underestimated by professors, being overlooked for scholarships, having people talk down to them, and the list goes on. But one thing I admire about the black students and all students at my school is that we don't let obstacles stop us from achieving.

Despite the challenges and/or discrimination you may face for being black or white, gay or straight, obese or underweight, tall or short, a student with a physical disability, or a student with a learning disability – I want you to know that it is still possible to overcome your struggles and rise to the **top**. Be aware that discrimination does unfortunately *still* exist. Do your best to be an advocate for change, peace, and acceptance for all types of people who you may meet in college.

12

Sexual orientation.

I played basketball in high school and had a few lesbian teammates, so I had been exposed to different sexual orientations besides heterosexual before entering college. However, I wasn't good friends with any homosexual or bisexual people, and I just felt indifferent about the topics of homosexuality.

Once I came to college, I had no choice but to face and take a stance on homosexuality. I had homosexual students in my residence halls, in my organizations, in my classes and homosexual professors & advisors. I believe that God placed people in my path whom I became close friends with and later found out their sexual orientation to show me that homosexual people should be treated just as equally as heterosexual people.

It breaks my heart to see students my age still living in denial of their sexuality because they fear the mistreatment that will come with expressing who they truly are. When you do encounter people of a different sexuality, imagine yourself in their shoes and treat them how you'd want to be treated. Simple as that.

13

Mental health.

Dancing on the way back to our dorm

I never realized what an issue mental health was – not only in college students, but also in Americans of all ages – until I came to college. College aged students have to deal with the normal stressors of life as well as the stressors that come along with being a college student – class work, finding themselves, making new friends, dating, adjusting to a new environment, finding jobs/internships, financial aid, peer pressure and more.

Since being in college, I've had two of my close friends tell me they wanted to commit **suicide**. And I've witnessed countless students struggle in silence. Mental health is a serious issue that shouldn't be ignored. If you feel overwhelmed in school, don't just push through it. Seek **professional** help. Every school *should* have resources so that you don't have to work through your issues alone.

14

Use your resources.

After I graduated from high school, I was super tempted to light a fire and burn all of the assignments, papers, quizzes and tests from the past four years. I was just so happy to be finished with that stage of life. Praise God I didn't!

I kept all of my old papers from high school and 75% of them have been useful in college. Unfortunately, college professors don't always teach the basics that you may have forgotten since freshman year of high school, and having those old resources will be extremely beneficial.

I also learned to use my human resources. If I took a class on a subject that I wasn't really comfortable with (or didn't really care about), I reached out to friends and classmates who maybe had a better understanding of the course. Learning from your peers can be just as effective as learning from a professor because we understand how one another think about information.

Peer pressure.

I'll admit that I was a little worried about the "peer pressure" you hear so much about when you go to college. It may be more present in certain organizations at your school, but overall there really isn't much peer pressure to do things you don't want to. Other students are in the same boat as you – they're going to school away from their comfort zones and are most likely too worried about fitting in themselves to pester you about doing something stupid.

I sometimes felt peer pressure from guys to do things that I wasn't interested in doing, but my strong foundation and friend group helped me avoid those traps. The key to avoiding peer pressure is being so mentally strong that you cannot be easily swayed. If you know what you believe and stand for, you won't fall for the clever words or tricks of others who may not have your best interests in mind.

Having a supportive and caring group of people around you is so important when it comes to peer pressure. You need to be surrounded by people who will tell you the truth and remind you of your morals when they may slip your mind.

16

Meet people who look like you.

 If you went to a high school where everyone looks like you, then your first instinct in college will probably be to flee to the first minority student you see who appears to be normal and friendly, right? My high school was only about 35% black, but I sought out some black friends once I got to Tech.

It's comfortable to be friends with people who understand your background without you saying a word. Race and ethnicity are silent qualifiers for someone who you may get along with. I understand this, and support it to an extent.

If you're black, you should absolutely meet other black people. If you're white, you should definitely meet other white people. But don't limit yourself and limit your college experience by never breaking out of your race bubble. I'm grateful for my black college friends because there are some experiences that only they can relate to.

17

Meet people who don't look like you.

I started college as a summer freshman. Looking back, it was probably the best decision I could have made concerning my college experience. It was so much easier to meet people since we took the same classes and lived in the same dorms.

Some of my first friends in college didn't look like me. They were white, Asian, or Indian. And since then, I've met people from over twenty different countries.

Meeting people who don't look like you usually means meeting people who don't think like you, didn't grow up like you, don't listen to the same music as you, don't talk the same way as you, etc. However, you'll be pleasantly surprised to find out how much you have in common with someone who has a vastly different outward appearance. I have learned the most about myself from my best friends who look **nothing** like me.

Get involved & love your school!

GT football field – Bobby Dodd Stadium at Grant Field

If you're not invested in your school, you probably won't get much out of your college experience – straight up. Just like anything else in life, you get back what you put in. Since I was barely accepted into Tech, I was just happy to be walking around campus and more than eager to get involved in organizations and attend as many events as I could.

Yes, I stay busy, and yes I **LOVE** MY SCHOOL! It's so sad to hear people speak down on their respective schools when these are supposed to be some of the best years of our lives. Regardless of where you end up going to school, take pride in your school and in your education. Attend sporting events, join clubs, start clubs, wear your school's apparel and enjoy the years when you can say that you **currently** attend the school you love so much!

Study abroad.

Studying abroad in Madrid, Spain

I studied abroad in Madrid, Spain the summer before my senior year. It's probably the most fun I've had in college. I lived there for about six weeks and also traveled to France, Italy and other cities in Spain. The group I traveled with was such a diverse mix of students and we all became so close after living and studying abroad together.

If your college offers the opportunity to study abroad, do it. There are scholarships available to help you pay for it, don't let the price tag stand in your way. I had a going away party and my family & family friends donated funds to make my trip possible.

I chose to study in Spain because the courses helped me complete my Spanish minor and I wanted to be completely immersed in the Spanish culture. The trip was life changing and opened my eyes to how other people outside of America live – so worth it.

20

Create a resume & portfolio.

Throughout high school I wrote down any activity I participated in, sport I played, or award I received. Little did I know, but I was basically creating an informal résumé. It's essential to have a résumé while you're in college. There are plenty of websites and resources for creating an appropriate and professional résumé, so be sure to create a version your freshman year and expand upon that version throughout college.

In addition to having a résumé, I also created a personal portfolio online. With everything "going digital," it's wise to have your credentials in a digital format. I used a blog website and made the title my name so that when employers search for me, my portfolio (which included my résumé) was one of the first results to appear. Employers view tons of résumés when searching for someone to fill a position, so your goal should be to stand out from the other applicants (in a good way)!

21

Meet your professors.

I'm not suggesting that you suck up to every professor; no one likes "that student." But, professors do appreciate students who are invested in their education and will typically respond positively to these students. I didn't learn this lesson until my second year in college – having your professors know your name and your face (for a good reason) is such a blessing.

You can only benefit from having professors who know and appreciate you. Once you start needing recommendations, internships, or jobs – you'll be so glad that you took the time to introduce yourself on the first day of class.

Even if a professor isn't teaching you a course, if you're interested in their area of study and expertise, reach out to them! I've learned that professors love students who love the subjects that they love. Makes sense, right? Always keep your relationships professional, but get to know your professor beyond the surface level and the outcome will most likely be in your favor.

22

Get to know your advisor.

The same thought process goes for getting to know your advisor. Depending on your school's size, your advisor could be responsible for over 100 other students. Most people I know only seek their advisor's help for scheduling issues or discussing graduation requirements.

But your advisor can be an even greater resource. Really get to know him or her and share your personal goals, collegiate goals, and career goals when you meet. If you're struggling with a class, say so. Once I started sharing what was going on in my college career with my advisor, she started sharing opportunities that I might be interested in.

She has helped me make decisions about my college career that I would not have been able to wisely make on my own, and for that I am very grateful.

Roommates.

The idea of a stranger as a college roommate can be horrifying. I know I was a little scared to move in with my first roommate who I connected with on Facebook. I knew she was Persian, short, from Georgia, and also liked *Grey's Anatomy*. Thank goodness she was normal! We got along well and hung out a little bit. We didn't become best friends or anything, but we're still in touch.

Don't freak out if you're not best friends with your roommate! You will meet other people. If your living situation isn't as comfortable as mine was freshman year, try to communicate your thoughts with your roommate, then your residence hall advisor if you're still not happy. Your living situation plays a large role in your academic success so you should be satisfied with it. Again, treat him or her how you want to be treated.

24

Black student organizations.

Members of GT black student organizations

I was involved with a black student organization my first three years of college and for good reason. BSO's allow for black students to more easily meet one another on a campus where we could easily feel alone.

I met the majority of my black friends through my involvement in BSO's. I also encourage getting involved with these organizations if you're interested in pledging a fraternity or sorority. Getting involved with these organizations also taught me more about my culture and history through special events and traditions with other black students. I fully support BSO's on campuses like Tech, but also support black students branching out to other organizations.

25

Predominantly white student organizations.

Student Government Association '11-'12 Executive Cabinet

While I have actively participated in BSO's, I also made it a **point** to apply for predominately white organizations (PWO's). I knew I was going against the odds and trying to be involved in something that would be a challenge for me.

At times it was frustrating being the single minority voice against the majority, but it made me a stronger leader. When there's no one else in the group to stand up for what you believe in, you have **no choice but to speak up**. I have learned from my white counter parts and they've learned from me. Getting involved with major campus organizations has allowed me to meet and really get to know campus administrators, including the president of Georgia Tech, on a personal level. I hope that I've also encouraged other minority students to join PWO's.

26

Changing your major.

I know people who have changed their major four times. And while I don't suggest doing this...just know that it's okay to change your mind.

Of course it's great if you know exactly what you want to major in before you start your first class and you keep that major until you graduate. Yet, things don't always work out that way. I changed my major after my first fall semester – my original major would have required too many computer science courses and I struggled through the intro course.

It was the best decision for me, because my new major was more focused on the media and communications aspects of technology – my true passions. Don't be frightened by the idea of changing your mind about your major. While your major won't necessarily define who you are or what career path you'll take, it will be a large deciding factor.

Also, be proud of your major. Liberal Arts students don't have the most respected majors at our school, but I have respect for my major and I'm proud of the path I've taken to pursue my career.

What to wear.

Dressed for game day

I can't possibly advise you on how to dress because fashion changes so often. But I will share that most people don't get too dressed up for classes (at most schools). When you visit your school, take mental notes of how people are dressed and that should give you some idea of the fashion norms.

I personally dressed in Nike shorts, jeans, t-shirts, etc. my first two years of school and dressed up for game days or special events. However, my junior year and this year I've been dressing in business casual just about every day because I typically have meetings with administrators for student government. I don't mind dressing up every day because my clothes actually get some use, but don't feel pressured to dress any way that makes you feel uncomfortable. Express yourself!

28

Finding your place.

As an orientation leader, so many freshmen expressed their fear of not "finding their place" or fitting in at college. I'm here to tell you that if you meet people, join organizations, embark on new experiences, and enjoy college; you will find your place.

It may not happen right away, but one day you will realize that you are the person you wanted to be in college. You'll realize that you're close friends with people who were strangers just a few years ago. You will have new goals and dreams. You will be passionate about a subject matter you knew nothing about in high school. And you will have discovered your purpose.

Don't force this moment of epiphany. It happens for different people at different times. When you do realize that you have **arrived** and you've "found yourself," celebrate!

With the Nu Mu Chapter of Alpha Phi Alpha Fraternity, Inc.

I made the decision to not join a sorority in college. I thought about pledging a NPHC sorority because I have Greek family members who encouraged pledging and I just always pictured myself doing so. However, after expressing interest, I quickly learned that Greekdom wasn't for me. And it's not for everyone.

I do have friends who pledged and who love their organizations, though. They've met incredible "brothers" and "sisters" because of pledging and have landed opportunities via networking within their organizations. You have to make the decision to be Greek or not. Just know that being Greek doesn't make you better than others nor does being a non-Greek. As long as you're happy with your decision, you've made the right one.

30

High school friends.

High school friend, Hannah, visiting my dorm

As my senior year of high school came to a close, I was definitely anxious and worried about how I would (or *if* I would) keep in touch with friends from high school. Most of my friends went to schools out-of-state while I went to school just 30 minutes away. I wondered how often we'd talk or when I'd see them again.

I will tell you that if both you and your friend make the effort to stay friends, you'll stay friends. Keeping up with high school friends definitely takes effort, and I'm learning that keeping up with college friends after they graduate takes even more effort. However, the effort is more than worth it when you need someone to talk to at 4am and the only person you want to hear from is your high school best friend.

31

Parents.

I've always had a pretty good relationship with my parents. Sure, we went through a few rollercoaster years while I was in middle and high school, but who doesn't? Yet, it wasn't until I went away to college that I realized how much they had done for me.

Your parents/guardians can be your biggest fans/supporters/motivators during college if you let them. It's easy to shut them out and just want to get away after 18 years or so of living under their roof with their rules. But, be careful when distancing yourself. I know that when I succeed or fail at something in school or life, my parents will **still** love me. They are proud of me regardless, and have a genuine interest in my life. For that I am forever grateful.

If you grew up with an alternative living situation, appreciate whomever it was that cared for you. Not everyone grows up the same way, and that's ok. Be sure to keep in touch with your family and loved ones who were there before college and they will be there cheering you on at the finish line (graduation).

32

Going back home.

People always ask me how often is too often to go back home. I think it depends on the person. Personally, I stop by my parents' house (for dinner) every week after working (at my high school job). Those visits home, no matter how long, always lift my spirits.

Seeing the people who love me the most and being in an environment that I've known for so long just relaxes me like nothing else. When I go home, it's an escape from the stressors of school and life in Atlanta.

I know going home isn't as easy for everyone. I have several best friends who are out-of-state students and I make sure to invite them home with me as often as I can so that they can enjoy the feeling of "being home" even if it's not with their family. So if you're going to school out-of-state, befriend some in-state students and you'll still get some home cooked meals every now and then!

33

Explore your city.

Going to school in Atlanta, GA is such a blessing. Our city is so beautiful and has so much to offer, but I don't think I've taken full advantage of the unique places in the city. It's easy to keep going back to the same places in your college's city once you find the spots you like. But, I challenge you to discover new places and fall in love with new stores, restaurants and venues.

Discover all that your city has to offer, no matter how large or small it is. Go on adventures with friends and learn about the history of your city and school. One reason I want to continue to live in Atlanta after graduation is because I don't think I've fully **lived** in Atlanta yet. I know there is still so much to see and I plan to see it before moving anywhere else.

Physical activity.

The "Freshman 15" is **REAL**. And it's more like "Freshman 30."

However, the weight gain is completely avoidable if you take the

necessary steps to be healthy in college. I definitely recommend you

have a plan to stay or get healthy once you get to school. Even small

steps toward being physically active are better than nothing.

I can't get myself to our beautiful gym on campus to save my

life. It just doesn't happen. However, since I know that I don't go to the

gym to work out, I don't take the public transportation at school. That

means **walking** everywhere. Rain or shine. Heels or flats. Heavy book

bag or light book bag. Walking to and from my classes and work has

helped me tone my legs over the years and keep the weight off. I also

make an effort to take the steps instead of the elevator, anything to build

in a work out during my daily routine.

Making healthy eating choices also plays a role in how healthy

you are during college. No one will be with you saying "nah, you can't

eat McDonald's at 3am." So you have to hear that voice in your head

and choose a healthier option when the temptation approaches you.

Romance.

Well, the title of this book is "Single Black Female…" so you can guess my relationship status. I may not have *profound* advice to offer in this area, but I have made some observations over the years. I have high standards when it comes to everything (males included), and honestly have yet to meet a guy I'd want to be in a relationship with.

I've gone on dates and gotten to know some guys but nothing serious. I've learned that many guys (especially black guys) have a mentality of playing in college and settling later. Even my close guy friends, who are great people, are still not interested in having a girlfriend. Meanwhile, some of my classmates are engaged or have already gotten married. I'm just trying to pass Calculus!

I'm happily single and happily waiting for the right guy. If you meet your husband or wife in college, that's fantastic! If you don't, also fantastic! Single life doesn't mean you're lonely, it just means you're still preparing to meet another person to share your love with. It would be a shame to settle for the wrong person too soon. Enjoy college and don't feel pressured to do anything too soon!

Partying.

Celebrating our friend Ellie's birthday

I like to party. I'm guessing my parents did too – I had to get it from somewhere! Some schools allow for more partying than others (Tech isn't really known for its raging parties), but we have our fair share.

No matter where you go, I guarantee there will be partying taking place. I fully support partying as long as it's controlled and people don't get hurt. Things get real scary when you have people blacking out from alcohol poisoning, passing out from drugs, being taken advantage of sexually or other awful outcomes that happen all too often because of drugs and alcohol. Remember the laws when you party and don't be upset if you get **caught** breaking the law.

Keepin' your social media classy.

Of course this section follows the "Partying" section. I can't believe some of the photos people tweet, upload to Facebook and Instagram and email out of them partying. Those photos never go away. It's not as bad if you're of age, but those photos can still be seen by the wrong person (future employers, family members, professors) and ruins your chances of an opportunity.

I often remind myself, and my friends to keep social media classy. Even if your profiles are private (which most of mine are), you still have to be careful. I ask myself, "would I be ok with my dad seeing this photo?" and if the answer is no, I don't take the photo nor post it.

More and more employers are doing internet searches of potential candidates and you don't want a profile picture of you doing a keg stand, smoking a blunt, twerking half naked, etc. to give them reason to turn your application away. Have fun, just don't feel the need to share everything with the entire the world (especially your not so classy moments).

38

Mentors.

One thing I wish I had done earlier in college is found a mentor. I know several students who have mentors both at Tech and outside of Tech who have provided inspiration and opportunities. Recently, I have found positive and established people to serve as mentors and I am very grateful for them.

Mentors can give you personal, professional and academic advice that parents and friends may not always be able to provide. Mentors are also people who you can look up to and aim to be like.

On the flip side, once you become a great student leader, be available to serve as a mentor for other students. I've been involved in organizations that automatically place me in the "mentor" position, and I've had the privilege of inspiring and loving other students. Being both a mentor and mentee has been life changing for me, and something I hope everyone can experience.

39

Accountability partners.

Posing with my best friend, Nick

Along with mentors, you also need accountability partners. I owe so much of my success in college and in life to the people who have held me accountable for achieving those successes. Often times, those people become your best friends.

Accountability partners are invested in your dreams and goals and invested in helping you make those dreams and goals realized. I had accountability partners for writing this book, for starting and continuing my blog and for completing school. You can only encourage yourself so much when you start to face obstacles and are tempted to give up. I'm grateful for all the people who refused to let me quit.

Moving off campus.

With my first off campus roommate, Jade

I started living off campus my fourth year in school and I have absolutely loved it. However, I don't think I would appreciate my new lifestyle as much if I hadn't lived on campus for the first three years of school.

I appreciate that I lived like a typical college student in residence halls and on-campus apartments. It wasn't the most comfortable living situation or the cheapest, but the experience made it all worth it. I now pay rent (ugh!) and utilities (ugh!!), but I'm happy with where I live and my roommate. It's a blessing having my own bedroom and bathroom after sharing these spaces with too many people over the past few years.

Scholarships & loans.

Apply, apply, apply for scholarships! Right now. I expected for scholarships to fall into my lap because I was smart, athletic and involved in high school. It did not work out that way. Luckily, I qualified for Georgia's scholarship for in-state students at in-state schools, but that is the only scholarship I received.

While I did apply for many scholarships, I should have applied for more. There are funds available for students in need, **so please don't let the price tag of school defer you from furthering your education**.

Loans are also available for students, and although it's not the prettiest option, loans are sometimes the only option. I plan to pay off my student loans as possible and I hope that the government will soon create a system that lowers the interest on student loans. I understand people not wanting to graduate in debt, but that fear is slowing our nation's progress.

42

Studying.

I never really studied in high school. Not because I didn't care, but because it wasn't too necessary. I crammed for the AP Exams and a few other big tests my junior and senior year of high school, but besides that I typically winged it and did well.

I'm not living the same life in college. I study. And I study **a lot**. The academic culture of every school is different, but at Tech we're pretty **serious** about academics. The students at our school were at the top of their classes in high school and now we struggle and stay up late (sometimes staying awake all night). Be prepared for a change in study habits and make friends with people willing to make sacrifices to succeed academically.

Energy.

I have become a coffee addict. Starbucks, QT, Dunkin' Donuts, McDonald's – I support all of them with my coffee habit. You'll need a source of energy when you get to college. Many people drink coffee, some drink tea, others exercise for energy and some people resort to drugs to stay awake. I suggest any but the later.

Drugs are so dangerous, especially today with people using lethal substitutions for products. The coffee, tea and exercise should be done in moderation, but are better than even a small dose of a drug you haven't been professionally prescribed.

I've heard horror stories of students overdosing on Adderall or similar drugs and having their hearts stop or even worse…dying. It's never worth it. Find a healthy way to stay energized and find friends to partake in these healthy energizers with you. Meet up with friends to drink coffee/tea and do homework. Work out with a friend at the gym. Just never sacrifice your health for a quick fix that could end up killing you. You won't need any energy if you're dead.

Budgeting.

You know why people always say college students are broke? Uh, because we are! It's too easy to BMF (blow money fast) when you're in college and not even realize how much you're spending. You'll spend money eating out (because that's how Americans like to meet up), going out, attending events, paying dues, buying books, paying rent (ugh!), shopping and more.

Older siblings, parents or responsible friends can help you create a budget. You'll have to put a limit on how much you spend on certain things per month or at least be aware of how much you're spending. Budgeting isn't always fun, but it does prepare you for the real world and force you to get creative when hanging out.

I started making smarter decisions and asking myself if I really needed something before purchasing it. Eventually, the money I saved was enough to make **major** purchases!

Having a car on campus.

Freshman year riding in Ericka's car

When my parents told me I couldn't take my car on campus for my freshman year, I thought I was going to die. How would I function without the car I'd been driving since turning 16? Haha, it's really not that bad. You'll make friends with people who do have cars on campus or find other ways to travel. Just know that you won't be **stuck** and bored out of your mind (which is what I predicted).

My friend Ericka had her car on campus freshman year because she was an out-of-state student who traveled home sometimes during the semester. I was allowed to have my car on campus starting my sophomore year so that I could drive to work. However, I have friends who are seniors who still don't have a car on campus, and they're getting by just fine.

46

Working while in school.

I've had a job at a law office since I was 16 (and still have that same job). So I'm definitely an advocate for working, but only if having a job doesn't interfere with your academics. Your school may have on-campus job opportunities that are flexible with your classes.

Also look into internships and off-campus jobs if you have the proper transportation. Good jobs and internship experiences are the perfect items to add on your résumé once you start applying for different opportunities later on in life.

I also work for the communications department at my school as an internship and it's been a phenomenal experience. I've met incredible communications professionals who have taught me small and large, yet equally valuable lessons. Having this job, along with my law office job has taught me time management skills, how to prioritize items and how to adapt to different working environments.

Run for something.

Two of my most memorable yet nerve-racking college experiences have been running for senior class representative and running for Ms. Georgia Tech (homecoming queen). I did become a senior class rep and by getting the most votes got the title of Class President. I made it to the semi-finalist round (top 10) for homecoming queen and was then cut.

Losing is never fun, but I wouldn't take back the experience for anything. When you run for something, you see who your **true** friends are, who truly supports you, what people **really** think of you, and what people think you stand for. I saw the true character of others revealed during campaigning for both events and I learned so much about myself by putting myself out there to be judged.

Though it was uncomfortable having people publicly judge and criticize whether or not I was worthy of being crowned, it was constructive and reminded me of why I love Georgia Tech. If you have the opportunity to run for something, do it. I promise you'll learn more about yourself and the people you think are your friends.

48

Plan for post-grad life.

It's never too early to start planning for post-graduation life. Don't assume that your plan will pan out exactly how you want it to, but it's useful to have an idea of what you plan to pursue after graduating.

College goes by quickly and before you know it, it's your final semester of college and people are constantly asking you "so...what's next for you?" The worst response you could have is, "Uh, I dunno."

Have some sort of plans or dreams for life after college. And remember, you can always continue your education by getting your Masters' and Doctorate degrees. I have dreams of earning both someday. I don't ever want to stop learning.

College bucket list.

This goes back to the first piece of advice, but a more fun version of knowing what you want to do. Create a bucket list of things to do in college. They can be specific to your college or the city you live in, or random things you'd like to achieve in life during your time in college.

A few items on my bucket list were to meet three "Bravolebrities" – I met **Andy Cohen**, NeNe Leakes and Ms. Lawrence (from Real Housewives of ATL), attend at least five concerts – I've attended over fifteen so far during college, and personally impact the lives of three other students. I'm happy that I've completed the majority of my college bucket list because that means it's time to make a new one. The best way to feel accomplished is to be aware of what you're accomplishing.

Leave your mark.

After being inducted into a leadership honor society, ODK

Going to college and graduating is great, but what's even greater is leaving your mark at your college. Make a difference and a positive change while you're in college. Become a mentor to another student. Give back to your school some how. Make a positive social change. When you cross the stage at graduation, you should cross knowing that you have left your mark and impact on your school's history. Regardless of how small or large that impact may be. Instead of just being a student who came and went...be a student who people remember and respect. Leave a legacy somehow, some way.

I also plan to stay connected to Georgia Tech after I graduate. Besides donating money (which is what they really want and need), I also want to physically come back, give back and be involved with my institution.

51

Discover your passion.

Your passion is what you can't go a day without thinking about. When you're doing something you're passionate about, it doesn't feel like work. I'm in love with my passions. When I'm doing communications work for Tech, student government or my personal blog – I feel happy. That's how I know I'm passionate about communications and want to pursue something involving communications for my career.

I have also become passionate about finding a solution to the major issues of homelessness and healthcare in Atlanta. Every day when I see a homeless man or woman on the street, I wonder what his or her story involves. And furthermore, I pray that I will one day be involved in creating a better life for them.

My current career plans are to be a communications specialist for a healthcare organization and/or hospital. I just want to help people. College will show you what matters most to you. Figure out a way to make your passions your career and you'll never work a day in your life.

52

Photograph it

Since joining the yearbook staff in high school, I've gotten into the habit of taking my digital camera with me everywhere I go. But it's a habit that I hope to never break. My little point and shoot camera has captured so many classic college memories over the years.

My friends pester me about uploading photos to Facebook after every event because they know I've probably taken some quality shots that will bring back great memories whenever they're viewed. I'm not telling you to join the paparazzi as a college student (that's doing the most), but definitely capture some of the moments. They fly by!

With Martin Luther King III

Get a job.

Once you have your passion and know what you enjoy doing – time to find a job! It's great to reach out to someone who has the career you want. Talk to him or her and get a better idea of what the job entails. Then, learn what it takes to get a similar job. I suggest researching jobs your junior year and applying for them your senior year. However, certain careers such as consulting start recruiting at the beginning of a student's senior year.

When you start applying for jobs, be prepared for rejection. Thousands of other students and other adults are applying for the same positions. Don't get discouraged if you don't hear back after applying for jobs. I always remind myself that rejection is a blessing and it wasn't meant to be.

You have a better chance of getting a job when you know someone involved in the selection process. If your school has a career service, use it! If your family member or friend knows someone in the field you want to enter, contact him or her. Research the company before your interview and dress to impress at your interview. **Make the company want you**.

54

Graduate (with recognition).

If you do what you're supposed to (go to class, do your homework, study, take the tests, etc.) you'll most likely graduate, right? So why not take it a step further and aim to graduate with some sort of recognition.

Graduating with recognition can be a difficult task at any school (especially at schools like Georgia Tech), but definitely possible. I admire the students at Tech who are committed to graduating with Honors, High Honors or Highest Honors. I am personally aiming for High Honors, which is a 3.3 or higher on a 4.0 scale.

Find out what the requirements are for graduating with honors your freshman year so that you can have a goal to work toward, and make the necessary steps for reaching that goal.

Certain organizations also award cords and pins for you to wear at graduation, another way to graduate with recognition!

We all reflect in different ways.

For me, writing is my favorite form of reflection. It's also great to discuss your college experience with older family members, younger family members, compare stories with high school friends and reflect with the people at your college who have gone through similar experiences.

I honestly can't believe I only have one semester left of college. I'm heartbroken that this chapter of my life is coming to an end, just like you're probably heartbroken that this book is coming to an end. But really, college is great – there's nothing else like it. I recommend it to anyone willing to grow, learn more about themselves and the world, and truly discover themselves.

I haven't been the perfect student. I don't have a 4.0 GPA. I'm not the most popular or most involved person at school. I'm definitely not the smartest person. **And that's fino**.

Attending college and allowing my experiences to empower me and change me for the better have made me into who I am today - a very **happy** young woman.

56

College has included many late nights (some all-nighters), countless cups of coffee, friendships made and friendships ended, smiles, tears, breakthroughs, accomplishments, failures and indescribable moments. The moments that have been too precious to put into words - those have been my favorite parts of college.

You'll understand what I mean when you start school and one night you realize that you're having the time of your life with people who you could have never met, had you not attended school.

College isn't just a time to get away from your parents and/or siblings. It's a really unique opportunity – a set of years – a limited time period – for you to transition into the real world.

Remember that happiness is a state of mind. Expect the unexpected and react accordingly. It won't be perfect, but everything that happens will play a role in the person you're supposed to be when you cross the stage at graduation. Congratulations in advance!

Every ending is another beginning.

Keep up with Vett.

Learn more about Vett, read more advice and keep up with her life by

reading her blog – Real College Student Atlanta, Inc.

Contact: rcsoatl@gmail.com with questions

Real College
Student of
ATLANTA
the *only* site for the
people of **Atlanta** and
college students/young adults
everywhere.

www.rcsoatl.com

Author biography

Vettica Kay Vandiver.

But she goes by Vett. Senior at Georgia Tech, living and learning in

Atlanta, GA. Vett started her blog, Real College Student of Atlanta, Inc.,

the summer before her senior year to promote a sense of community in

the Atlanta area & encourage higher education.

She's passionate about life – and **living** it to the fullest.

60

23319697R00034

Made in the USA
Lexington, KY
06 June 2013